HANUKKAH

A CROWELL HOLIDAY BOOK

HANUKKAH

BY NORMA SIMON

Illustrations by Symeon Shimin

THOMAS Y. CROWELL COMPANY · NEW YORK

CROWELL HOLIDAY BOOKS

Edited by Susan Bartlett Weber

HANUKKAH

All over the world each year, Jewish mothers polish the family Menorah, the Hanukkah lamp, until it gleams. Now is the time to prepare for Hanukkah, the Festival of Lights.

Hanukkah begins on the 25th day of the Hebrew month of *Kislev*. On the Roman calendar this day falls at the end of November or some time during December.

Jewish children love the Menorah with its small candles that burn the eight nights of Hanukkah. The bright lights remind them of the Jews' fight to pray to one God in their own way.

The story of Hanukkah begins more than twenty-one hundred years ago in Judea. There the Jewish people lived and worked.

At that time, Antiochus the Syrian ruled Judea. He wanted the Jewish people to pray to the Greek gods, as he did. But the Jews had prayed to their one God, Jehovah, from the time of Moses, and they refused.

Antiochus decided to punish them. He said they would be put to death unless they gave up their Jewish religion.

Antiochus sent his soldiers to the villages and cities. They burned the Jewish holy books and ordered the Jews to pray to statues of the Greek gods. They placed a huge statue of the Greek god Zeus in the Jewish Temple in Jerusalem.

Some Jews liked the Greek ways and wanted to give up their Jewish religion. But most Jews chose to die if they could not pray to one God. They could not forget the ways their fathers had taught them.

The Jewish people were in grave danger and in great need of help. Then one day a leader appeared. He was an old Jewish priest named Mattathias, who lived in the village of Modin with his five sons.

When the king's soldiers marched into Modin, they ordered Mattathias to pray to the Greek god. The bearded priest shouted, "No!"

But one of the fearful villagers said, "I will pray to the Greek gods."

Mattathias turned red with anger. He seized a sword from a nearby soldier and killed his fellow Jew.

When the soldiers tried to stop him, he fought them with all his might. His strong sons and many of the people of Modin fought, too. At last, after a terrible battle, all the king's men lay dead.

Mattathias gathered his people around him. "Whosoever is for God, let him follow me!" he commanded.

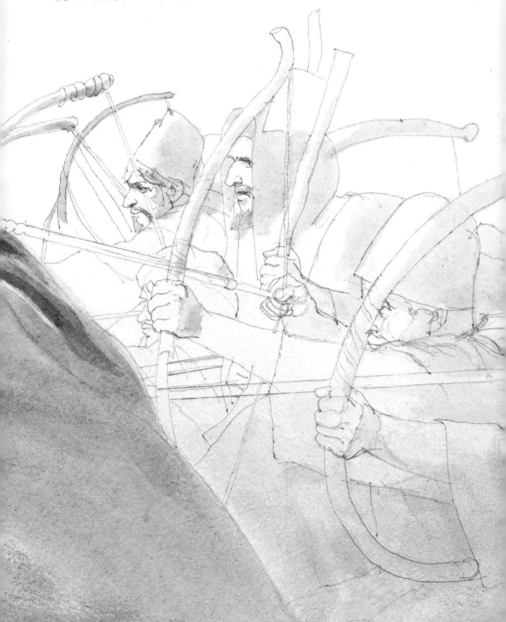

Mattathias and his sons quickly fled Modin and hid in caves in the mountains. Many villagers left their homes to join the Jewish fighters.

For a long time Mattathias was the leader of this small band of brave men. Whenever they could, they fought against the Syrian soldiers. Finally, Mattathias grew too old to fight, and his son Judah took his place.

Mattathias and his sons were called the Maccabees. *Maccabee* means "hammer" in Hebrew, the language of the Jews.

Jews from every part of Judea followed the Maccabees. But, even so, there were far more Syrian soldiers. Judah Maccabee had to be a wise and clever general.

He led his army in small surprise attacks. Before the enemy could strike back, the Maccabees and their men disappeared into the hills.

The Jewish army grew tired from long years of hard fighting. But all weariness was forgotten the triumphant day they captured Jerusalem, the capital of Judea, from the Syrians.

Judah and his army destroyed the many statues of the Greek gods in the Temple. Then they carefully made the Temple a house of prayer to their one God again.

The day the Temple was ready the Maccabees proclaimed a holiday to last eight days. They were celebrating their victory and the restoration of the Temple. They called the holiday *Hanukkah,* which means "dedication" in Hebrew.

From that time on, each year, Hanukkah was celebrated for eight days with joy and gladness. The story of Judah and his army became part of the history of the Jews.

Much later a legend grew to be part of the Hanukkah story, too. No one knows exactly how it began.

On the first Hanukkah, the legend says, the priests wanted to light the Temple Menorah. To the Jews, light was always part of celebrations to God.

They looked in the Temple for jars of the olive oil they needed to burn in the lamp. But they found only one small jar with enough oil for one day. It took eight days to make new oil. There seemed nothing they could do.

So, the first day of Hanukkah the precious oil was poured into the lamp. It should not have burned more than one day.

But on the second day it was still
burning. On the third day the oil was
still burning. And even on the fourth
day the oil was still burning.

It seemed like a miracle.

Each day the oil kept burning. On the
eighth day, when the new oil was ready,
the Menorah was still bright with light.

To many people now, the miracle of the oil is the reason for celebrating Hanukkah. To others, the Maccabee victory over Antiochus and the restoration of the Temple are the reasons for celebration, just as they were for Judah and his army.

The sons of Mattathias were leaders of the Jews the rest of their lives. As the years passed, Jewish families scattered to other lands near Judea. Still later, some of them settled in Poland, Russia, Hungary, and Rumania.

Wherever they went, they carried their religion to their new homes. Every year, their children and children's children celebrated the festival of Hanukkah.

Many of the Jews in America today come from families who once lived in Poland, Russia, Hungary, and Rumania.

Among the things their families brought to America from the Old World were beautiful Hanukkah Menorahs. These Menorahs burned oil in small cups.

Now most Menorahs hold thin wax candles. They are made of wood, brass, copper, or silver. A few are made of gold.

The Hanukkah Menorah has nine cups for candles. Eight of the candles stand for the eight days the oil burned in the legend of the first Hanukkah. The ninth cup is different.

The ninth cup holds the shamos candle. *Shamos* means "servant" in Hebrew. Each night the shamos is lit first. Then it is used to light the other candles.

One more candle is added each night. Each night the candles burn all the way down.

One candle and the shamos the first night; two candles and the shamos the second night; three candles and the shamos the third night; and one more each of the other five nights. The Menorah burns brighter and brighter.

In Jewish homes the eight nights of Hanukkah begin with the lighting of the candles. The family recites blessings in Hebrew or in English. One of the blessings is: "Blessed art Thou, O Lord our God, King of the Universe who has hallowed us with his precepts, and who has commanded us to kindle the lamp of Hanukkah."

Every night the lighted Menorah is placed on the window sill so that all who pass may see the burning candles.

During the holidays pounds of potatoes are peeled and grated for making pancakes, or *latkes*. Friends and relatives are usually invited to a latke party. Eating latkes with sour cream or applesauce is an old Hanukkah custom.

Gifts of money, or *gelt,* are an old custom, too. The night the first candle is lighted, the Hanukkah gelt is given to the children. Some parents give a small gift each evening.

Every night, after the meal, comes a time for storytelling and games. The children listen to the exciting story of Hanukkah. Then they play a very old game, "spinning the dreidel."

The dreidel is a top which was once made of lead or clay. Today it is usually made of wood or plastic. It always has four sides.

On each side is one Hebrew letter: Nun, or N; Gimel, or G; Hei, or H; Shin, or Sh. These are the first letters of the Hebrew words: *Nes Godol Hayah SHam.* They mean: "A great miracle happened there."

With a twist of the fingers the dreidel is spun. The children call out the Hebrew letter on top as the dreidel stops turning and falls on one side.

Nuts and raisins are the prizes for the game. The spinner wins them with some letters and loses them with others. Everyone takes turns spinning the dreidel and nibbles the nuts and raisins he wins.

Neighbors and relatives come to visit and play card games. They tell stories about other family Hanukkahs and sip tea. They eat honey and sponge cakes and dried fruit. Young and old voices join in the singing of *Ma'oz Tsur,* a Hebrew hymn which tells of the bravery of the Jews.

Many children go to Hanukkah parties at their synagogues. They sing holiday songs in Hebrew and in English. They give plays and act out the ancient story of the Jews' fight to pray to their own God. Judah Maccabee is always the hero and Antiochus is the villain.

In one country in the world, Hanukkah is a holiday for all the people. Judea, the old land of the Maccabees, is called Israel now. It is the homeland of the Jews again and Hebrew is the national language. The Jewish holidays are the national holidays, just as the Fourth of July and Labor Day are in the United States.

There, during Hanukkah, huge Menorahs are lit. They shine from high watchtowers, from synagogues, and from the tops of city halls.

People travel to Modin, the town of the Maccabees. They visit caves where the Jewish soldiers hid many centuries ago.

Like the Maccabees, most people want the right to pray to God in their own way. This right is called freedom of religion. People of all religions have come to the United States of America for this freedom.

The first Jewish families came to America from Spain and Portugal. Some settled in Newport, Rhode Island.

After a visit to Newport in 1790, George Washington, the first President of United States, wrote a letter to these Jews.

He wrote that freedom of religion was the right of all citizens of the United States. He hoped that people of all religions would live side by side in peace. No one here need be afraid, he said, to worship as he pleased.

ABOUT THE AUTHOR

Norma Simon is particularly interested in the field of child guidance, and she has taught in nursery school, in kindergarten, and at the Vassar Institute for Family Living.

She received a B.A. in economics from Brooklyn College, and undertook graduate work in early-childhood education at the Bank Street College of Education and in psychology at the New School for Social Research.

Mrs. Simon enjoys a wide range of activities including cooking, gardening, modern dance, and folk music. She lives with her husband and three children in Norwalk, Connecticut.

ABOUT THE ILLUSTRATOR

Symeon Shimin was born in Astrakhan, on the Caspian Sea, Russia, and came to the United States with his family ten years later. He attended art classes at Cooper Union in the evenings. Mr. Shimin painted for a while in the studio of George Luks, but he is primarily self taught and found his schooling for the most part in the museums and art galleries in this country and in France and Spain.

In 1938 Mr. Shimin was chosen to paint a mural in the Department of Justice Building in Washington, D.C. Recognition and many invitations to museum exhibitions followed, including those at the Whitney Museum of Art, the Art Institute of Chicago, the National Gallery in Washington, D.C., and the National Gallery in Ottawa, Canada. His paintings are in public and private collections.

Jews in America are now a part of American history. They have become part of the history of every country where they have lived.

They have shared the spirit of Hanukkah, the Festival of Lights, with all people who love freedom.